CW01024128

Not Dead But Sleeping
By Anna Della Subin

10.28.2017

FOR ALEX,

THIS WORLD IS NOT OUR WORLD —
TO THE CAVE!

YOURS,
ANNA DELLA

Triple Canopy

Not Dead But Sleeping, primarily edited by
William S. Smith with Triple Canopy.

Published by Triple Canopy, New York, 2017.

ISBN 978-0-9847346-9-6

Printed by Shapco Printing, Minneapolis, MN, USA

triplecanopy

264 Canal Street, 3w
New York, New York 10013
canopycanopycanopy.com
Triple Canopy is a nonprofit 501(c)(3) organization

For Hussein

A sarcophagus in the Coemeterium of the Seven Sleepers at Ephesus, Turkey, 1940. Photograph by Nicholas V. Artamonoff. Courtesy of Dumbarton Oaks. The cemetery is a sleepery, *koimētērion*, from the Greek—a place to be laid to sleep.

*There is nothing more tragic than to sleep
through a revolution.*
—Martin Luther King Jr., 1965

*We shall not all sleep,
but we shall all be changed.*
—1 Corinthians 15:51

Sleepers awaken in the Coemeterium of the Seven Sleepers at Ephesus, 1940.
Photograph by Nicholas V. Artamonoff. Courtesy of Dumbarton Oaks.

Contents

11   Introduction
       By William S. Smith

19   1. The Actors
35   2. The Picklers
49   3. Zzzzzzzzzzzzz [The Caves]
71   4. Revolution and/or Apocalypse
97   5. Resurrection

109   Sources
121   Figures
139   Acknowledgments

Introduction
By William S. Smith

"Everyone here is awake," one young Egyptian activist told the *New York Times* in a 2011 report on nightlife in Tahrir Square, the unofficial capital of the Arab Spring. Who could sleep when there were slogans to be written, strategies to debate, news to discuss, poetry to recite, music to be played, and food to be prepared for thousands? The protester's sentiment was echoed in a line of graffiti scrawled on the side of a tank: "The revolution is in Tahrir; no sleeping in bed."

Revolution and sleep seem, intuitively, to be antithetical forces. When Anna Della Subin first undertook this book, in 2013, she proposed that sleeping be understood as a revolutionary act. For various reasons, this appeared to be incongruous with the conditions of life and politics in Egypt, which had partly inspired her research into Tawfiq al-Hakim's 1933 play *The People of the Cave* and the story on which it is based. (The story, in which seven Christian youths fall asleep for three centuries only to awaken in a radically transformed world, is present in many cultures and religions, but it is particularly prominent in Islam.) The ouster of Hosni Mubarak had animated a previously moribund political system, turning it fluid and malleable. The country looked like it was up for grabs. Sleep seemed like an indulgence or a distraction.

Revolutionaries throughout history have expressed disdain for sleep. Nikolai Chernyshevsky, the nineteenth-century Russian revolutionary and an archetype for twentieth-century ascetics wedded to the cause, allowed himself to sleep only grudgingly—and when he did rest it was on a bed of nails. For Walter Benjamin and Guy Debord, the sleeper is a figure of complacency, and nodding off invariably means accepting the status quo. Subin quotes Martin Luther King's famous admonishment not to sleep through the revolution.

Yet the sleeper, too, has a historical mandate. Coverage of the protest movements, revolutions, and occupations that have focused the world's attention in the past five years is replete with iconic images of marching bodies with raised fists. But spend any amount of time reading about those uprisings, encampments, and mass mobilizations, and you'll discover a vast archive of images of repose.

Amid the buzz of Tahrir Square, protesters fell asleep at all times of day and night, sometimes napping in the shade of tanks. In Istanbul, they curled up beneath Turkish flags and posters of Atatürk in the tent city erected at Gezi Park. In Hong Kong, they sprawled beneath umbrellas on financial district highways, gumming up traffic. Recumbent, snoring bodies are just as effective "upon the gears and upon the wheels, upon the levers, upon all the apparatus," as Mario Savio said in 1964, at making the machine stop—if only for the night.

In 2011, Occupy Wall Street activists undertook "sleepful protests," making beds of tarps and sleeping bags on the sidewalks of New York's financial district. #SleepOWS became one of the many fleeting hashtags associated with the movement, which shaped Subin's disquisition on the power of slumber and influenced her understanding of the legacy of the people of the cave. The ceaseless marches and seminars and committee meetings were stoked and fortified by the quieter—but no less radical—act of falling asleep in public. One reporter described sleep as a ritual of OWS with a social dimension, "sleep, lying among your comrades, everyone vulnerable, everyone absurd, stretched out between the coffee trucks and the police cruisers, under the watchful eye of a mobile NYPD surveillance tower jacked up over a truck."

The collective passing out of young people in the financial hub of the city that never sleeps might be seen as an affront to what the critic Jonathan Crary calls 24–7 capitalism. The sleeper reclaims her right to rest contra contemporary working life, which hinges on the regulation of her body and her schedule in accordance with the whims (and on-demand systems) of employers, as well as on her free time being devoted to the indulgence of manufactured desire.

Subin reanimates numerous episodes in the history of the sleepers. She draws from a number of sources: sacred texts like the Qur'an, modern political histories like that of the Civil Rights movement, and contemporary artworks like the Egyptian artist Wael Shawky's *The Cave* (2005).

In her account, sleep marks a rupture in the continuity of experience. Subin's sleeper-heroes range from the mythical shepherds of ancient Rome who snooze through the empire's embrace of Christianity to the legendary Rip Van Winkle, who remained unconscious through the American Revolution, to Julian West, an otherwise hapless Bostonian who dozes through the arrival of Edward Bellamy's nineteenth-century socialist utopia. These figures are wholly ignorant of the historical changes that have taken place while they slept, which makes them astute social critics. Equipped only with the common sense and the received wisdom of their time, they are forced to confront radically altered bodies of knowledge, beliefs, and prejudices.

Not Dead But Sleeping

1. The Actors

It appeared as a satire in a Cairo newspaper just as the nineteenth century pirouetted into the twentieth. A pasha, dead for fifty years but recently resurrected from the grave, took his seat in the audience at the Khedivial Opera House with his companion, a hapless writer who had been out for a walk in the City of the Dead at the wrong moment. The writer had been contemplating death—an attempt to find inspiration for his book—when suddenly the tomb of Egypt's former minister of war had opened up not far from where he stood. As Muhammad al-Muwaylihi imagined in his serialized epic, *Hadith 'Isa ibn Hisham*, the formidable pasha, naked except for his burial shroud, demanded the writer's coat, and the two set out for a livelier neighborhood. They went to the theater, an entertainment newly popular within Cairene society since the pasha's time. Waiting in the audience, they watched as men of all ages laughed and hurled insults at one another, occasionally waving to the ladies in the harem boxes who glimmered faintly, like planets. The curtain rose. Seeing the look on the appalled pasha's face, the writer explained that drama was a medium imported from the Occident, and Egyptians, in their laziness, hadn't bothered to become good at it. The pasha rushed out of the Opera and back to the writer's house, where he crawled into bed. But he couldn't sleep after such an unbearable play. His reanimated brain was racing too fast.

Fig. 1.1

YAMLIKHA: This world is not our world. …

MARNUSH: What do you mean?

YAMLIKHA: Do you know how much time we spent in the cave?

MARNUSH: A week? A month, according to your fantastic calculation?

YAMLIKHA: Marnush, we are dead! Ghosts!

MARNUSH: What are you talking about?

YAMLIKHA: Three hundred years.

On the night of December 12, 1935, Egypt's National Theatre Company had its first performance at the Khedivial Opera House. For its inaugural run, the company chose *Ahl al-Kahf*, or *The People of the Cave*, written in Arabic by Tawfiq al-Hakim. At the opening of the first act, three men and a dog awaken in darkness inside a cave. Their limbs are numb, and their backs ache against the chill of the stone floor. Was it all a dream? The young court ministers Marnush and Mishlinya, along with the shepherd Yamlikha, had fled for their lives from the city of Tarsus after the pagan king Dikyanos discovered their crypto-Christian faith. They hid in the mountains; overcome with exhaustion and sorrow, they wept themselves to sleep. Was it all a dream, the dream of three somnambulists on the run?

In a haze, the men argue over how long they have slumbered, "a day, or part of a day?" [*They are lit only by blue stage lights; their shadows are enormous.*] Famished, they send Yamlikha out for food, but he returns bewildered and empty-handed. He relates how, when he tried to offer a coin to a hunter he met along the road, the man was astonished at his appearance, and his horse recoiled in fright. Turning over the piece of silver in his palm, the hunter demanded to know whether Yamlikha had found some long-buried treasure. Soon after, a crowd of villagers bursts into the cave, and the light from their torches floods the stage, fully illuminating the actors. "Ghosts! The dead!" the villagers shriek, aghast at the sight of their matted robes, never-ending beards, and fingernails uncut for three hundred years.

The men and the dog Qitmir are carried from their crypt to the palace. To their amazement, the symbol of the cross is openly displayed in Tarsus; a Christian emperor, Theodosius, is in power; and the men are received as saints. [*The throne room is set with Byzantine columns, mosaics, and bas-reliefs depicting birds, and is suffused with yellow light.*] Amid these overnight transformations, Mishlinya is relieved to see the face of his betrothed, Priska, the tyrant Dikyanos's daughter, who had converted for him in secret. But Priska, still wearing the gold crucifix he gave her, does not recognize Mishlinya, and shrinks away in fear. After receiving haircuts, shaves, and clean but strangely styled clothes, the men—well preserved in the cool, dark cave—appear young again. Venturing out of the palace, Marnush attempts to locate his family, but finds an arms dealership in place of his home. Searching for his infant son, he uncovers a dilapidated grave, with an inscription telling that the boy died a war hero at the age of sixty. The shepherd Yamlikha fails to find his flock.

Distraught, and thoroughly persuaded that three centuries have passed, Yamlikha and Marnush conclude that they cannot live in this new world. "We are like fish, whose water has changed from sweet to salty," Marnush protests, as they slip back to the cave and into the exile of sleep. But Mishlinya, unable to accept that this Priska is not *his* Priska but her descendant, stays behind in the world of the awake. As she tries to convince him of the oceanic night that divides them, Mishlinya falls into a frenzied state: "Priska! My darling! Come … You are she … Oh, God, you're not she … Am I asleep? Am I alive? Am I in some muddled dream?" But then again, ruminates the sleeper, she never seemed as beautiful as in the dream …

Fig. 1.2

It might have seemed an appropriate play with
which to inaugurate the National Theatre,
for everywhere it was said that Egypt, having
fallen behind the times for several centuries,
was at last awakening into modernity. After an
indolent, five-hundred-year nap in the shade,
Egyptians had been seized by new spirits:
of nationalism, cultural revival, and the promise
of prosperity. A new age had dawned—not
only in Egypt but across the Arab world—called
the *Nahda*: the "Awakening," "Resurrection,"
or "Renaissance." The birth of modern Egyptian
theater coincided with this rousing of the
nation's consciousness. Though it had counted
indigenous traditions such as the medieval
shadow-puppet play, Egyptian theater in the
European style had only begun in the mid-
nineteenth century. As the European presence
grew, theaters sprang up across Cairo and
Alexandria, where one could find Italian opera
and French comedies, as well as Egyptianized

24

adaptations in Arabic. Molière's *Tartuffe* became *Shaykh Matluf*, and Hamlet did not die. In 1869, to celebrate the opening of the Suez Canal, the Khedive of Egypt, Ismail Pasha, commissioned the magnificent Khedivial Opera House in Cairo. Egyptians had developed a taste for the theater, but as the undead pasha—awakened by the noise of the Awakening—discovered, it required a cacophonous mix of hysterics and tears.

The man who would become known as the father of Egyptian drama—in part through the sheer number of plays he churned out—by his own account came into the world silently, sometime between 1898 and 1903. (He liked to invent different birth years to suit various purposes.) The son of an eminent Egyptian judge and an infamously overbearing Turkish mother, as a child in Alexandria Tawfiq al-Hakim was fascinated with the world of the unseen. At night he would find himself awake, keeping watch for the jinn who acted out their own dramas in the family house. He was convinced he had oracular powers, startling his family when his prophecies occasionally came true. His auguries were not grand or world-historical, but generally limited to predictions of the movements of his relatives, of which he had many. Once, when a telegram arrived stating that his uncle had suddenly died, the young Tawfiq declared to his distraught parents that it was not true, and that his uncle would soon reappear. Moments later, his undead relative walked through the door.

In 1919, as a student in Cairo, al-Hakim wrote his first full-length play, *The Unwelcome Guest*, inspired by the revolution of that year. He joined Egyptians across the country in revolt against their unwelcome guests, the British, and was briefly jailed. While studying law in the early 1920s, al-Hakim continued to moonlight as a playwright, signing his work with a pen name to escape the censure of his parents, who, like many at the time, disapproved of the theater. When he discovered his son's secret, al-Hakim's scandalized father sent him off to Paris to pursue a doctorate in law, reasoning by a curious logic that he would be kept far from the stage. On his return to Cairo three years later, he was without a degree but had seen every play imaginable— from Ibsen, Shaw, and Maeterlinck to Chekhov and Pirandello—and had written more of his own. Settling back into life in Egypt, al-Hakim felt disoriented and profoundly changed. He was like a man from another time who had arrived in a sleeping land, as he wrote despondently to a friend. In this state of disillusionment, he composed *The People of the Cave*. Stuck in his job as a lawyer and fearing the repercussions of revealing his clandestine craft, he waited five years before publishing it.

He had been listening to Beethoven's Fifth Symphony as he wrote, and modeled the four acts of the play on the symphony's four sections. But he had purchased the records, unlabeled and out of order, at a stand in Paris, and never had the chance to hear the symphony in a concert hall. Al-Hakim would put on the second, andante movement thinking it was the first, and wrote the slow dialogue of the first scene of *The People of the Cave* to resemble it, speeding up the pace in the following acts. It was not until years later that he realized his mistake. Time was out of joint.

Fig. 1.3

In 1928, the year al-Hakim wrote the play, Mahmoud Mukhtar's iconic statue of the *Nahdat Misr*, or the "Awakening of Egypt," had just been unveiled in Cairo. The granite statue, depicting a peasant woman throwing off her veil and rousing a sleeping sphinx, urged the nation to face a new dawn. Everywhere, from Egypt's newspapers to the coffeehouses that al-Hakim frequented, a question was posed: How should the forward-looking nation become modern without losing touch with its past? The debate took on a related shape among the literary elites: Should Egyptian literature look for inspiration to its storied former lives? And if so, which of its many epochs should it appropriate: the glory of the pharaohs, the philosophy of the Greeks, the erudition of the Abbasids, the poetry of the Mamluks? Or should it awaken fully to the present and look toward new art forms—the innovations of Europe—to create a literature that would speak to the contemporary age? Al-Hakim's resurrected saints seemed a fitting parable. But at the end of the script, the somnolent martyrs decide they cannot exist in the present day. They slink back into the cave, sacrificing their chance at a second life. Was the play an indictment of the relic Egypt's rush to keep up with the modern world? Yet to condemn it would implicate the new form of the drama itself. In the stage directions, al-Hakim indicated that the final act, as well as the first, should take place entirely in darkness.

When *The People of the Cave,* after five years' sleep, appeared in print in the spring of 1933, al-Hakim was fired from his job. His text was hailed in literary circles as a major landmark in Egyptian letters. "This was not a revolution against a heritage but the actual beginning of that heritage," the critic Ghali Shukri wrote; "Egyptian drama was born in its near-perfect form with *The People of the Cave.*" Egypt's foremost intellectual, the blind luminary Taha Hussein, declared, "I have no hesitation in saying that it is the first story created in Arabic literature that can be called a real play." But it was not entirely successful; Hussein reproached al-Hakim for "shocking errors in language," and *"ugly mistakes, some of which violate the essence of Arabic."* He chided him for disregarding the experience of the audience by making the work too long in places, and concluded that it was not yet everything he hoped to see Arabic drama achieve. Expressing concern as to what would happen when this drama of ideas was performed on the stage, Hussein suggested he take over the task of perfecting the draft—an offer al-Hakim declined.

Taha Hussein's premonitions were not unfounded: By most accounts, the inaugural production, which went up two years later, was a resounding flop. In a review in the newspaper *Al-Ahram*, Abd al-Rahman Nasir remarked, "This story, as you have seen, is soft in its depth, calm in its revolution of thought. How does it appear to an Egyptian audience used to the violence and drama of the Grand Guignol?" To an audience hungover from melodramas and musicals, the play's metaphysics were too lofty, its formal Arabic dialogue too stiff, and the thought experiment required of them too tiring. "It reminds one of a lecture rather than a play," remarked one critic. It was no more exciting than watching balls thrown back and forth, complained another. Commentators pointed out that the script was interminably digressive. Why must the actors ramble on about the Japanese fisherman Urashima, who went to sea in his boat and returned four hundred years later? People in the audience fell asleep.

Al-Hakim waited until the fourth night to see the show. Afterward, much like his characters,

the man from another time fled the stage. Though
he published a letter in *Al-Ahram* congratulating
the National Theatre's director, the renowned
poet Khalil Mutran, on a triumphant success, in
private al-Hakim would tell friends that he had
been kept away from the rehearsals, was dismayed
by what little he saw, and had asked before opening night for the play to be withdrawn. Hurled
into a crisis of doubt about his abilities as a playwright, he wrote, "The chasm between me and the
stage has deepened." In the years that followed, he
convinced himself that he had never created *The
People of the Cave* with the intention of having it
staged. His theater, he concluded, could exist only
in the mind, with the actors as symbols, moving
freely in the realm of ideas. Though he would go
on to write more than seventy plays, few were
staged in the following decades, and the National
Theatre was hesitant to undertake further produc-
tions. As its director confessed to al-Hakim, "Do
you know what I do before deciding about a play
by you? I read it at home to my children, and if
they don't fall asleep, I take it on."

Had al-Hakim's sleepers returned too early
in Egypt's dawn? The same year the play came
out in print, he also published his much more

widely praised novel *The Return of the Spirit,* an allegorical tale about the emergence of an authentic, Egyptian leader who would rouse the nation's soul. (The story, rather immodestly, was based on the author's own childhood.) Gamal Abdel Nasser credited the book with turning him into a revolutionary. In September 1935, as the National Theatre was in rehearsals, the precocious seventeen-year-old Nasser wrote in a letter to a friend, "We have frequently spoken of a great action that would bring a dramatic change to the nation and awaken it from its slumber. But nothing has been done yet."

Twenty-five years later, the National Theatre restaged the play in an anniversary production. *The People of the Cave* was reanimated in a changed world: Nasser and the Free Officers had exiled the king, expelled the British, seized foreign businesses, and forged alliances across the Arab world. In a speech marking the nationalization of the Suez Canal, Nasser declared that the Arab spirit was now *"fully awakened* to its new destiny." In his role as president, he hailed al-Hakim as "Reviver of Literature," and presented him with honors usually reserved for heads of state. But once again, during the 1960 performance few could stay awake. Though al-Hakim's text was secure in its place in Egypt's canon, popular consensus again deemed the play a failure. "I am trying to do in thirty what has taken the theater in other languages about two thousand years," al-Hakim despaired. "Authorship is martyrdom in this country."

Fig. 1.4

In bed, unable to sleep, the undead pasha called out for the writer, who was in the middle of a dream in the next room. The writer rushed to the pasha's bedside, and they spent the rest of the night deep in conversation. They spoke about society and politics and art, about what had changed for the better and what for the worse, until the dawn began to hold funeral rites for the night. Night had been a beautiful woman, wrote al-Muwaylihi, too beautiful to suffer either veil or shawl. She toyed with the stars that shone with clarity around her décolletage, then tore them off. She ripped the two orbs of Ursa Minor from her ears, and pulled off from her slender finger the ring of the Pleiades. Her youth fading fast, she became a shaky, gray-haired old woman, leaning on the cane formed by Gemini. Soon dawn covered her with a blue sheet, and morning, in her white raiment, moved in. Night was dead, but it was as if all the world were displaying how life persists in her absence, as it does in ours. Birds flew up over the body of the night. The pasha, it would turn out, was a figment of the writer's dream.

2. The Picklers

And when ye withdraw from them and that which
they worship except God, then seek refuge in the
Cave; your Lord will spread for you His mercy and
will prepare for you a pillow in your plight.
— Qur'an 18:16

In a prison cell in Cairo, Sayyid Qutb, the
Egyptian ideologue and Muslim Brotherhood
member, wrote a thirty-volume commentary
on the Qur'an. He completed it in 1965, the year
before he was executed. For Qutb, incarcerated
for a decade, the eighteenth chapter of the Qur'an
had a particular resonance. It told how a group of
Christian youths, fleeing religious persecution,
had escaped into a cave and fallen asleep for 309
years. God, speaking directly to the Prophet
Muhammad, relates how He sealed the sleepers'
ears so that no sound would disturb them, and
inscribed lead tablets at the entrance so that
all would know their story. In Qutb's reading
of the *Surat al-Kahf*, the claustrophobic cave
was unexpectedly comfortable. "The surprise
here is great indeed," he wrote. "These young

believers who have abandoned their people and
families, forsaking all the pleasures of this life
and preferring instead to sleep rough in a small,
dark cave, begin to sense God's grace. They feel it
coming, easy, comforting, abundant, limitless."
The narrow walls of the chamber were thrown
back to reveal a wide horizon, and the loneliness
of the sleepers was dispelled by His mercy. *We
caused them to turn over to the right and to the left*,
God narrates. He flipped the sleepers periodically
from side to side, so that they wouldn't suffer
bedsores. There was no one protecting them but
God, Qutb wrote.

> *And thou mightest have seen the sun, when it rose,
> inclining from the cave towards the right, and, when
> it set, passing them by on the left, while they were in a
> fissure of the cave. That was one of God's signs.* (18:17)

The Prophet grieved at how his message was
scorned by the Meccans, wrote the young
Indian nationalist leader Abul Kalam Azad. God
told the story of the sleepers to console him—a
portrait of those who, unwilling to renounce the
truth, bore adversity heroically. Azad was working
on his Urdu commentary and translation of the

Qur'an from a jail cell in Ranchi; beginning in 1916, he was imprisoned for several years for editing newspapers that condemned the British Raj and called for independence. He became a committed disciple of Gandhi, espousing nonviolent resistance. When he was freed, only to be soon locked up once more—this time with his papers destroyed—Azad began again his work on the Qur'an. In verse 17 of the eighteenth sura, God reveals how He shifted the path of the sun at sunrise and sunset to avoid shining into the mouth of the cave, lest the sleepers' bodies decay in the heat. Were one to have peered inside, *Thou wouldst have deemed them waking though they were asleep.* They were not sleeping but temporarily dead, Azad argued. They were so absorbed by their prayers that death caught them in postures of worship. The cave was open on two sides; cross-ventilation kept their bodies cool but caused them to sway. Anyone who stumbled upon them would have found a terrifying sight.

In the 1935 production of *The People of the Cave*, the director added a prelude to draw out the connection between the play and its Qur'anic inspiration. It was a story that everyone in the Khedivial Opera House audience would have

recognized, for in Egypt, the *Surat al-Kahf* is
memorized in schools and recited in mosques.
Children are taught that seventy thousand angels
stand guard around the words of the chapter.
The play began in darkness; from an unknown
direction a sound broke the silence and slowly
grew louder—the voice of the renowned chanter
Shaykh Ali Mahmoud, singing the familiar
sura. The shadows of the three Christians were
projected onto the stage, caught in the act of secret
prayer. This was followed by scenes depicting
the torture of the Christians by the polytheists,
punctuated by eerie bursts of music. Then the
shadows acted out the flight to the cave, black
ghosts who moved behind an illuminated white
screen. In the final act of al-Hakim's script, the
sleeper Marnush, as he lies in the cave awaiting
death, radically renounces his religion. Battered
by the waves of time, Marnush dies "stripped of
everything," he declares. "Naked as I was born …
No thoughts, no emotions … and no faith." The
National Theatre Company, fearing controversy
for portraying one of the sleepers as an apostate,
omitted the lines from the play.

In the Qur'an, the story begins with a
question: *Or dost thou think the Men of the Cave*

and the inscription were among our signs a wonder?
(18:9) Al-Hakim's Cairo audience, in its unim-
pressed reaction, may well have been channeling
God's own attitude toward the sleepers. It was
not much of a miracle, the verses seem to say. We
can find among God's signs on earth much more
wondrous things than a long nap. Toward the end
of the story, a line reads, *Say, "It may be that my
Lord will lead me unto something nearer to guidance
than this"* (18:24). The twelfth-century Persian
scholar Shaykh Tabarsi wrote, "Its meaning is, Say,
perhaps my Lord will give to me from the signs
and the indications of prophecy, something that
will be closer to guidance, and better evidence,
than the story of the Men of the Cave." Azad, too,
warned against reading too much into the story.
Even Qutb, locked up in his own dark cell, wrote,
"Strange as their history is, it is not particularly
marvelous among the miracles and signs given by
God. Indeed there are numerous things that are
much more miraculous in the universe than the
story of the cave people." All they did was sleep.
The divine word itself seems to say, *Can't we find
something better than this?*

Fig. 2.1

The Qur'an raises an eyebrow at what was first a Christian tale. The oldest extant record of the story is found among the seven hundred homilies of the immensely prolific Syriac poet and bishop Jacob of Serugh, who died in 521 AD. Jacob, drawing on an older, unknown source, narrates that the sleepers awoke in the reign of Emperor Theodosius II, who ruled Byzantium from 408 to 450, the year before the poet himself was born. He locates the story not in Tarsus, the setting of al-Hakim's play, but in Ephesus. A further account is found in the Syriac version of the lost *Ecclesiastical History* of Zacharias Rhetor, originally written in Greek at the end of the fifth century, and included in the work of John of Ephesus, who lived between 507 and 586. The story appears in Latin in Gregory of Tours's *De gloria martyrum* around 571; Gregory credits his account to a Latin translation of a Syriac version—quite possibly of a story first told in Greek.

The legend of the sleepers travels north in the work of the eighth-century Benedictine monk Paul the Deacon in his *History of the Lombards*. In his retelling, they are Teutons who are still sleeping in the farthest, iciest reaches of northern Europe—seven future apostles destined for unbelieving countries. In the thirteenth century, the tale of the sleepers spread widely in the medieval best seller *The Golden Legend*, a collection of hagiographies compiled by the Italian archbishop of Genoa, Jacobus de Voragine. The legend reappears among the tales of *The Thousand and One Nights*, which al-Hakim's mother would read to him before bed every evening. It turns up in 1781 in Edward Gibbon's monumental *History of the Decline and Fall of the Roman Empire*, wherein the curmudgeonly English historian attempts to disentangle the conflicting transmissions of the story. Muhammad "has not shown much taste or ingenuity" in inventing the dog, the detours of the sun, and the divine flipping of the sleepers, Gibbon complained.

Some will say: they were three, their dog the fourth. Some say five, their dog the sixth. Many say seven. (18:22) Jacob of Serugh claims there were eight. Zacharias Rhetor says six. The medieval geographer Yaqut cites thirteen. *Say, O, Muhammad, My Lord knows best their number. None knoweth them save but a few.* "The impossibility of history as 'what actually happened' becomes the theme," wrote the California sage Norman O. Brown. "The Sleepers; how many were there? Lord only knows." Nor is there consensus as to how many years they slept. One version of Jacob's homilies cites 372 years; a second version, 350. It happened in a single long night, miraculous or not, beginning at some point during the reign of the tyrant Decius (249–51), until a moment in Theodosius's rule, which would give a figure closer to two centuries, not three. In the tenth century, the Patriarch of Alexandria Eutychius in his *Annals* gave a count of 149 years. In the Qur'an, God awakens the sleepers so that they might speculate on this very question. Was it *a day, or part of a day?* (18:19) The verses conclude, *Only God knows how long they have tarried.* And then He gives the answer: *They remained in the Cave for three hundred years, to which another nine may be added.* Gibbon is indignant: "Nothing less than the ignorance of Mahomet or the legendaries could suppose an interval of three or four hundred years," he scoffs, and gives a tally of 187 years. Or is it God who has no sense of time?

> YAMLIKHA: Maybe we've been here for a month?
> MARNUSH: You're mad! A month? And what did we do all this time?
> YAMLIKHA: We slept.

Fig. 2.2

"The night is a curtain and the day is a stage," declares the undead pasha, after he decides to stop despairing of the world he was resurrected in and laugh at it instead. The story of the sleepers may all been a play. In the year 447, Stephen, a priest in Ephesus, usurped the episcopal see of the archbishop Bassian, and threw his rival into prison without trial. The legitimacy of Stephen's coup was soon contested by the other archbishops, and Theodosius sent officials to Ephesus to investigate the affair. In order to consolidate his grasp on power, some say Stephen concocted a scheme: He would make his bishopric the site of a sensational miracle, one that would end any doubts as to whether God approved of his new regime. Sometime in the summer of 448, the archbishop may have invented and spread the story that seven martyrs, who had hidden in a cave during the persecutions of Decius, had just awoken, consecrating his diocese with their soporific grace. Some scholars suggest that he may have even hired seven young Ephesians as actors, who were to pretend they had just woken up in the deep future.

At the time, a doctrinal controversy was raging in the church as to whether the bodily rising of the dead was possible or not. It was a question with consequences for understanding Christ's resurrection, and our own future reanimation at the End of Days. As the Vatican scholar Ernest Honigmann suspects, Stephen may have commissioned the writing of the *Hypomnemata*, a Greek "memorandum" on "the veritable resurrection of seven youths," to record for posterity the miracle and refute the heretics who would say that the physical raising of the dead is impossible. Although no version predating Jacob of Serugh survives, scholars surmise that it may be the Greek source from which scribes like Jacob and Gregory of Tours learned the story. In the treatise, dedicated *in maiorem Stephani gloriam*, it is the bishop himself who finds the lead tablets at the entrance of the cave, proving the truth of the miracle, and the bishop who first realizes that the hand of God is at work. Indeed, Stephen is presented as possessing such godly foresight that he seemed to know of the miracle before it even happened.

While the story traveled and gathered many believers along the way, the miracle itself may have failed to achieve its purpose. Stephen's reputation never recovered, and his name was omitted from later versions of the *Hypomnemata* and from retellings of the tale. If he is remembered by history at all, it is as an embarrassment to the church. On the other hand, his rival, Bassian, is venerated among certain sects as a martyr who renounced his position and fled rather than adopt what he saw as the heretical decisions of the Council of Chalcedon in 451. At the council, Bassian and Stephen aired their grievances against each other, and both were condemned as illegitimate and corrupt, though no one questioned the resurrection of the sleepers. "Nobody would have dared to utter open doubts concerning a recent miracle which, though extraordinarily taxing to the credulity of believers, had certainly deeply impressed great masses of the faithful," writes Honigmann. But one of the council members made what seems to be a discreet allusion to it, "intelligible only to other skeptics; this can of course only be conjectured with due reserve," the scholar warns. When the question was debated as to where the next, legitimate bishop of Ephesus should be consecrated, Diogenes of Cyzicus argued that it should happen in Constantinople, rather than Ephesus, to avoid further controversies. For in Ephesus, Diogenes mused, "they consecrate the *salgamarius*—and that is the reason for all the trouble." A *salgamarius*, from the Latin, is one who makes or sells pickles.

Fig. 2.3

A flopped play, not quite a miracle, an old bishop's ruse. *Can't we find something better than this?* God Himself thinks we could. But inside any cavernous rock, we find a nest of sleepers. Al-Hakim thought his drama could exist only in the mind. Yet politicians and pilgrims have avidly desired this same story to exist in space. Beyond Ephesus and Tarsus in modern-day Turkey, more than forty caves, in countries from Tunisia to China to Azerbaijan, compete for the claim to the original darkness that pickled the sleepers. It is a point of national pride: State-funded archaeologists labor to prove that their nation's cave is the real one, while ministers of tourism promote the hollows as must-see attractions. The myth is contagious, like a global yawn. They slept and slept, awoke, and dozed once more. Can a story, one so often told, be a failure? Something about it is unsatisfying: We tell it because it is so. For fifteen hundred years, storytellers have been trying to improve on it, adding details, dialogues, subplots, and love interests. Still the legend falls flat, and still we try to resurrect it. Perhaps it is not a story at all, but a reaching toward one, like a zombie rising from a grave. Forever in the future is the dawn.

3. Zzzzzzzzzzzz [The Caves]

They slept the sleep of Endymion, but the moonlight, unrequited in her love, could not reach them. They slept in the place of the Dormition; they slept while Mary Magdalene, from her grave, kept watch. They slept while the great temple to Artemis was sacked. They slept surrounded by a vast necropolis of believers, believers in them. They slept near St. John; having dreamed the Book of Revelation, he lay in imageless exhaustion. Above his tomb the cracked earth rose and fell, in rhythm; his breath scattered the dust.

In 1869, Mark Twain posed for pictures in the ruins of Ephesus. "We do not embellish the general desolation of a desert much," he wrote. "We add what dignity we can to a stately ruin with our green umbrellas and jackasses, but it is little. However, we mean well."

They slept not in Ephesus but in Afsus, a town in Elbistan. They slept not in Afsus but in Fis, the village in Turkey where the Kurdish separatist group PKK was founded. "The cave that is in Ephesus does not comply with the definitions of the Qur'an," declares KurdishSaladinTV, a YouTube channel. "Since Saladin [Fis] is officially recognized as the cave of Seven Sleepers."

They slept in Amman, argues a scholar from Amman, who has done extensive research on this subject. In 1961, Jordanian archaeologists unearthed the jaw of the dog Qitmir, with one incisor and four molars intact.

They slept by the side of the Silk Road in Xinjiang, while raisins dried in the sun. They slept in a cave that once belonged to the Buddha. Some call it Apsus. When the Red Guards came to destroy the shrine, it is said a dog singlehandedly drove them off.

They slept in Maimana, in northern Afghanistan, in a cave lined with hundreds of handprints traced in chalk. Clusters of white tombstones surround the entrance, indications of those who came to visit, or to join them. Some say the Buddhas to the southeast in Bamiyan were once the pagan tyrant Dikyanos and his consort, turned to stone in an act of divine punishment. Further retribution was exacted in March 2001, when the Buddhas were dynamited by the Taliban. They slept on the outskirts of Paphos, where

Aphrodite rose from the sea. Seven relics were found in the cave, variously claimed to be the seven martyrs or the fossilized remains of seven Cypriot dwarf hippopotamuses.

They slept in Nakhchivan, in the shadow of the Ilandag, a mountain whose peak was chipped by Noah's Ark after the floodwaters receded. In the cave, no trace of the sleepers remains, except a meteorite worn smooth by the hands of pilgrims.

They slept in a nest in Tarsus, transformed into young birds. They fell asleep in Glastonbury, under the Chalice Well. They were weary from building a church out of twigs.

The whole of Europe thus, in one sense, answers the description of the cave, according to the website of the Lahore Ahmadiyya sect.

They slept in Gandia, south of Valencia, and in the hills of Granada at Loja. They slept in the crypt of the Marmoutier Abbey. They slept in every house on the Comoro Islands.

They slept in Chenini, in southern Tunisia.
When they awoke they were thirteen feet tall.

They slept in Marseille and in N'Gaous and in
Nabk, in the monastery of Saint Moses the
Abyssinian. They slept in the sky above Basra.
The only sound was the footsteps of centuries
entering and exiting the stage.

They slept over Damascus, in a cave on Mount
Qasioun. The caretaker of their shrine carries
a talisman: a photograph taken in the cave in 1954
of Louis Massignon, the Christian Islamicist
who spent his life hunting traces of their sleep.

They slept in Vieux-Marché in Brittany, and in
the cemetery of Guidjel, near Sétif. They were lost
in God as they slept.

They slept in Tibhirine, south of Algiers, where
seven French monks were beheaded in the night
in 1996. They slept in Midelt, in Morocco, with
their hands crossed in prayer, near the monastery
where the surviving monks fled.

They slept in Yemen, in the mountain sanctuary
of Jebel Saber, kept cool by a wind from the north
that rushed through the underground tombs.

They slept in Finland, where they are feted each
year on *Unikeonpäivä*, National Sleepyhead Day.
The last person in the house to awaken is thrown
into a lake. Or the left side of his chest is shaved.

They slept in Cairo in the crypt of al-Maghawri,
once occupied by the Bektashi Sufi order and
now by the Egyptian military. They slept through
the call of the muezzin who cries, *Prayer is better
than sleep.* They slept on the marble altar of the
Siebenschläferkirche in Rotthof, in positions of
overwrought repose.

Had you seen them, you would have fled in fear. (18:18)

They were called Maximian, Malchus, Martinian, Dionysius, Constantine, John, and Serapion. Or Clemens, Primus, Laetus, Theodorus, Gaudens, Quiriacus, and Innocentius. Or Arshaledes, Diomedes, Eugenius, Dimatheus, Bronatheus, Stephus, and Cyriacus. Or Maksimilina, Mashilina, Martunus, Yamlikha, Dabriyus, Sirabiyun, and Afastatiyus. Or Aleekha, Muksulimta, Tub-yunus, Udurgut, Yunus, Yuanus, and Kushfootut. Or Maximianus, Dionysius, Exacustodianus, Constantinus, Jamblichus, Johannes, and Martinianus. Or Maximilianus, Dionysius, Amulichus, Martinus, Antoninus, Johannes, and Marcellus. Or Maximilien, Marc, Martini, Denis, Jean, Séraphim, and Constantin. Or Gormánudr, Frerm, Hrútm, Einm, Sólm, Selm, and Kornskurdarmánudr. Or Dom Christian, Brother Luc, Father Christophe, Brother Michel, Father Bruno, Father Célestin, and Brother Paul. Or Adam, Idris, Noah, Abraham, Moses, Jesus, and Muhammad.

They made themselves a bed in your ear and went to sleep.

And the night grew long and old and miraculous.

And their dog (18:18)

It followed them as they fled. They drove it away with stones and branches, but it returned. They beat it nearly to death when, according to the Prophet's companion ibn Abbas, the dog spoke: "What do you want from me? Do not fear treachery from me: I love the friends of God." Qitmir remained awake all those years, with neither food nor water, keeping vigil while they slept.

The dog was yellow. It was black and white. The stern thirteenth-century theologian ibn Taymiyya listed the color of Qitmir among Those Things That Cannot Be Proved and Are in Any Case Useless, alongside the part of the cow struck by Moses and the size and type of wood of Noah's ship.

The dog was a man. Qitmir was Ali, the martyred son-in-law of the Prophet, appearing to the young men to test their faith. Or it was the Prophet's companion Salman al-Farsi who appeared in canine form. The dog became the star 80 Ursae Majoris.

After God revealed their story to him, Muhammad wanted to visit the sleepers, but He would not permit it. The angel Gabriel told him to seat the four future caliphs, Abu-Bakr, Omar, Osman, and Ali, on the four corners of a carpet, and let a strong wind carry his envoys to the cave. When they arrived, they loosened the rocks blocking the entrance to the cave and the light burst in. Qitmir leaped to his feet and greeted the caliphs.

The dog signaled, "Come in!"

They sleep near the navel of the sea, to which
all waters find their way. To reach them, one must
traverse the land of frost. They sleep in a subterranean citadel, uninfluenced by time. They sleep
while ships are flung into the nearby whirlpool
like arrows through the air, while Hvergelmir,
the roaring kettle, swallows them or spits them
back. They were put to sleep by inserting a
svefnthorn into each ear. Until the sleep thorns
fall or are taken out, the seven men will slumber.
They doze until Ragnarök, the day the gods
will die.

The sleepers are metalsmiths; they rest surrounded by their own creations, weapons built for
humans of supernatural size. They are cyclopes.
Bands of Frisians and Danes tried to plunder the
cavern, but when they touched the sleepers the
thieves' limbs withered and shrank.

They are the seven sons of Mímir, the guardian
of the middle root of the World Tree. They are the
four stags that graze off its branches: Dvalinn,
the Dormant One; Dáinn, the Dead One; Duneyrr,
Thundering in the Ear; and Duraþrór, the Snorer.
Each son is a seasonal change felt by the tree

each year; each ensures the seasons follow one another in their proper order. But when Mímir was slain in the wars between the god clans, the World Tree, having lost its caretaker, succumbed to the spell of time. It decays in crown and root; its deterioration is both natural and moral.

They have a sister, Nat, who takes care to see that they are shrouded in darkness at all times. Voices of other women, too, are heard in the tabernacle of sleep.

The *Vita Ædwardi Regis* records that on Easter Day, King Edward the Confessor sat at a banquet in Westminster surrounded by his bishops and nobles yet barely touched his dinner. He was immersed in thought. Suddenly, to the astonishment of all those present, he broke into "indecorous laughter." Soon his face clouded over again and his nobles asked him the reasons first for his merriment and then for his sadness. Edward replied that he had been thanking God for the abundant food and drink on his table, when God sent him a vision. Edward saw—as if he were there himself—the seven sleepers, lying inside a cave in Mount Celion near Ephesus. Suddenly, all the sleepers flipped over onto their backs, from the right side to the left, and Edward laughed at the synchronized sight. But he soon realized what it meant: For as long as they lie on their left side, violence and misery will plague the world.

On hearing this, Earl Harold summoned a knight, a clerk, and a monk to visit the cavern of the sleepers. And so it was, just as Edward had seen. The Ephesians maintained that they heard from their grandfathers that the seven had always slept on their right; but when they entered the cave

with the Englishmen, they were found to be lying
on their left. It was an omen of what was to befall
Christendom, on the eve of the First Crusade.
By the end of the eleventh century, Ephesus was
seized by the Seljuk Turks; it was wrested back
by Byzantium, only to be conquered again a
century later. "Whenever sorrow threatens, the
Sleepers turn on their sides," wrote the mythogra-
pher Sabine Baring-Gould.

They were drunks, according to Mark Twain.
They stole forty-two bottles of an aged liquor
from the grocer and drank them all. Their motto
was "Procrastination is the thief of time." They
fell asleep in the cave with their neighbor's
dog Ketmehr. When they awoke—stark naked—
they found that Ephesus had been radically
transformed and all their relatives were dead.
Strangers shut their doors on them in suspicion.
When the men realized they had been asleep
for two centuries, they exclaimed, "Behold, the jig
is up—let us die." Writes Twain, "The Seven-up
did cease in Ephesus, for that the Seven that were
up were down again, and departed and dead
withal. And the names that be upon their tombs,
even unto this time, are Johannes Smithianus,

Trumps, Gift, High, and Low, Jack, and The Game.
And with the sleepers lie also the bottles wherein
were once the curious liquors; and upon them
is writ, in ancient letters, such words as these—
names of heathen gods of olden time, perchance:
Rumpunch, Jinsling, Egnog. ... I know it is true,
because I have seen the cave myself."

They are not three or seven but thirteen, records the medieval geographer Yaqut, a freed slave from Baghdad. In 632, 'Ubadah ibn al-Samit was sent by Abu Bakr on a proselytizing mission to Byzantium and visited the cave. An iron door was unlocked for him, and he was led inside the chamber. Thirteen men were lying on their backs, in gray cloaks and knee-high leather boots. Ibn al-Samit related, "We uncovered their faces, one after the other, and lo! in all was the complexion of healthful bloom. There was red blood in their cheeks; some had grey hair and some had black." Each year, their caretakers would trim the sleepers' nails, cut their mustaches, and stand them upright to shake the dust from their clothes. "When we came to the last of the men, we found that his head had been cut off with the stroke of a sword," ibn al-Samit recalled, as recorded by Yaqut. "It was as though it had happened that very day." The caretakers related that after a band of invaders seized the cave, one of them demanded to know the story of the bodies. Disbelieving it, he severed one of their heads as an experiment. Mujahid ibn Yazid, who visited ninety years after ibn al-Samit, recorded that the wound of the headless sleeper still bled.

Ali ibn Yahya, on his own visit to the cave, relates
that he tried to smooth some rumpled hairs on
one of the sleepers' heads, but found they would
not flatten. The astrologer Muhammad ibn Musa
suspected a trick. Sent by the caliph al-Wathiq
to investigate the condition of the sleepers,
the caretaker at first refused to let him in, claiming
that harm would befall him. Ibn Musa persevered,
and entered the cavern to inspect the bodies,
which he noted were preserved with unguents,
aloes, myrrh, and camphor. He passed his hand
over their chests and hair. "We had imagined
they would have been living men, with the sem-
blance of those who are dead; but behold these
men are not of this sort," the astrologer complained to the caretaker. They were not sleeping
but embalmed. When ibn Musa resurfaced into
the daylight, the caretaker served him lunch. The
meal made the astrologer violently ill.

"Every morning, toward the dawn, very early,
they come down from the sky and visit that place
where they had slept, and then they go up again,"
said an Alawite woman to an interviewer in the
late 1990s. She lived near the cave at Tarsus, where
al-Hakim set his play. They were seven brothers,

the nephews of a cruel pharaoh who had forced
them to toil without rest. They decided to flee, and
meeting a shepherd, a dog, and a camel along
the way, hid in a cave in the hills of Enculus, where
they fell asleep. When they awoke, and realized
that a crowd had gathered around the cave, they
refused to leave it and prayed for help. God turned
them into the stars of the Big Dipper. Reports
circulate in Tarsus of a shaft of light emanating
from the constellation down to the cave.
"Once, on a summer night, I was sleeping on the
roof," related the woman, "and when I woke up
I saw them—really or not—I saw them in the
direction of the cave; there they came down. I do
not really know how. But they say it's like that,
so they say. The constellation is like a coffee pot.
If you stay until night I'll show it to you."

Others say the sleepers are the crew of the
constellation *Safina*, or Argo Navis, the ship that
hovers above the South Pole. Sailors once set
their courses using the star that formed its rudder,
Suhayl, or Canopus. A boy went exploring in
the cave and never came out, the Alawite woman
recalled. The police sealed the entrance so that
others would not get lost.

"Was it a dream?" wrote Danilo Kiš in a short story from *The Encyclopedia of the Dead.* "Was it a dream, the daylight, the light that streamed in on him when the people moved away from the entrance to the cave, when a door opened up in the wall of the crowd standing round, and a new light appeared, incontestably divine, a forgotten light, far and near at once, the light of a sunlit day, the light of life and clear sight?"

It was Yamlikha who was chosen from among them to venture out for food. On the road leading to the city, he saw white banners written with God's name. He rubbed his eyes with his hands. "Am I really awake?" This is how the story is told in an undated handwritten manuscript found in a cave in Tuyoq in Xinjiang province and now in the possession of the Finno-Ugrian Society. Yamlikha went to visit his old home, and found that several youths and an old man were living there. He greeted them, then informed them they were living in his house. The youths wanted to start a fight, but the old man restrained them and asked Yamlikha to tell his story. On hearing it, the old man laughed and lost consciousness. When he woke up, he said, "I am the son of your

son; you are my grandfather." He embraced
Yamlikha and wept. Then the old man said, "I
have a father who is very old, so old that he is
only skin and bone. I have wrapped him in cotton
and put him hanging in a litter. He is still alive."
He brought down the litter and, uncovering
it, carefully unwrapped the ancient man from the
cotton, "in the same way as a newborn child
would separate for the first time from his mother."
The old man brought milk and put it to the
mouth of the ancient, who drank the milk and
opened his eyes. He looked at his father's unwrin-
kled face and cried.

The Abbasid caliph al-Mu'tasim, who reigned from 833 to 842, had heard the rumor of the people of the cave and sent an emissary to Byzantium to search for them. His ambassador returned instead with a bundle of ancient Greek manuscripts. As Louis Massignon relates in his history of *les sept dormants*, some say the envoy discovered the texts near the bodies of the sleepers themselves, hidden in the same dark crevices. A team of scholars in Baghdad was devoted to translating them into Arabic. Al-Mu'tasim had inherited the project of preserving and translating Greek texts—long after they had been forgotten or destroyed in the West—from his predecessor, his half brother al-Ma'mun, who once met Aristotle in a dream. It was through the efforts of the Abbasids that much of the ancient knowledge was recovered. Via Baghdad, preserved in Arabic, Greek learning would later enter Europe, where it would be reclaimed as its own epistemological heritage.

In 448, the year that the questionable Bishop Stephen may have hired actors to pretend they had awakened—or the year when they really did resurrect—Theodosius issued an edict that all non-Christian books be burned. History forever repeats itself: Fearing the persecution of a Christian tyrant, pagan Greek texts fled to the hills.

They were men. They were books. They slept in caves.

4. Revolution and/or Apocalypse

In June 1965, Martin Luther King Jr. delivered the commencement address at Oberlin College. He titled his speech "Remaining Awake Through a Great Revolution." "I'm sure that you have read that arresting little story from the pen of Washington Irving entitled 'Rip Van Winkle,'" King began. "While he was peacefully snoring up in the mountain, a revolution was taking place in the world. … And Rip Van Winkle knew nothing about it; he was asleep." In Irving's tale—written over the course of a sleepless night in June 1818—the heroically lazy, henpecked Rip takes a twenty-year nap on the slopes of the Catskills. When he awakens, he finds that the village inn that once displayed a portrait of King George III now boasts the face of a different George, his friends are gone, and that other "petticoat government," the matriarchy of Dame Van Winkle, is dust. Rip is bewildered. "There are all too many people who, in some great period of social change, fail to achieve the new mental outlooks that the new situation demands," King warned. "There is nothing more tragic than to sleep through a revolution."

A profound transformation was under way in America and the world at large, King continued: the process of decolonization and the rise of the civil rights movement. He condemned those who would impede it. "Anyone who feels that our nation can survive half segregated and half integrated is sleeping through a revolution," he declared. Anyone who feels that we can live in isolation today … is sleeping through a revolution." And "anyone who feels that the problems of mankind can be solved through violence is sleeping through a revolution." Rip Van Winkle, in King's view, was on the wrong side of history— the side that snoozed. But although Rip slept through America's struggle for liberty, in Irving's tale he has a certain perspective that everyone else lacks. Due to his long slumber, he is uniquely able to compare two disparate moments, oppressed colony and newly independent nation, and see how they measure up. "The very character of the people seemed changed," Rip observes. "There was a busy, bustling, disputatious tone about it, instead of the accustomed phlegm and drowsy tranquility." It seems obvious, even innocuous, to put two instants side by side and see what has improved and what is for the worse. But in periods of upheaval this very mode of comparison has been a most controversial act. Sleepers are assessors of our awakenings. And sleep cannot be censored.

Fig. 4.1

The sleeper is the ultimate social critic, though he has missed most of what happened. In exile in Aleppo in 1929, a year after al-Hakim composed *The People of the Cave*, the Turkish intellectual Refik Halit Karay wrote the play *Deli*, or *Mad*. Maruf Bey, a man living in the Ottoman Empire, mysteriously becomes catatonic two days before the Young Turk Revolution in 1908, and comes to his senses twenty years later, to find that the sultanate and the caliphate have been abolished, Mustafa Kemal (later known as Atatürk) is in power, vast sociocultural and political reforms have been implemented, and his wife and daughter are dead. He is confounded by the changes that have taken place in his absence: a world war, new national borders, new methods of keeping time, short haircuts and education for women,

men without beards, the shuttering of Sufi lodges, saints' tombs, and madrassas, strange alterations to the Turkish language. "Am I misunderstanding something?" Maruf exclaims in confusion. "Surely I haven't recovered yet, I'm still sick, maybe I am mad. ... Or else everyone else has gone mad, and I'm the only one left who still has my senses!" He wonders whether he is in some muddled dream.

Atatürk's reforms were one answer to the question posed by al-Hakim's drama: how the nation, awakening into a new global order, should keep pace with modernity while holding on to its own character. Karay's play was radical for even imagining the Turkish Republic in continuity with the empire that preceded it. The play was essentially highlighting the obvious: There had been a rupture between past and present, a profound restructuring of society and culture in Turkey in a shockingly brief period. But in the 1920s and '30s, few authors were speaking to the overwhelming ambivalence, sadness, and absurdity that accompanied Turkey's abrupt modernization. Karay wrote in exile from a society in which stating the obvious was not allowed, as the scholar Christine Philliou has argued. In *Deli*, which was not published in Turkey until after Atatürk's death, Karay hinted that the changes the president had forced onto the country were, in many ways, mad. Egypt, once a part of the Ottoman Empire, was watching; Cairo pundits debated Turkey's swerve toward modernity and argued over whether it should be emulated. A diplomatic crisis between the two nations exploded in 1932 when Mustafa Kemal demanded that the Egyptian ambassador remove his fez—the old, venerable symbol of the ancien régime, which Turkey had outlawed—at a state dinner.

Surfacing from his torpor, Maruf Bey, whose name means "Mr. Common Sense," is the only one of Karay's characters who remembers his nation's past. But on the stage of history, another cast of sleepers expressed their dismay. In 1930, a dervish named Mehmet from the Naqshabandi Sufi order led a violent uprising against Atatürk's secularizing reforms and what he saw as the idolatry of the state. He declared his seven disciples the Seven Sleepers of the Cave and proclaimed himself the Mahdi, the prophet who, in the End of Days, will come to redeem the world gone awry. From Manisa in the west, Mehmet and his followers traveled to Menemen, outside Izmir, picking up a dog they called Kitmir along the way.

In the central mosque, the sheikh announced his return as the Mahdi, showed Kitmir to the congregation as proof, and declared that an army of seventy thousand was en route. Mehmet called for the restoration of the caliphate and Islamic law, the reopening of Sufi shrines, and a return to old ways of life. When local army troops attempted to suppress the revolt, a hundred of Mehmet's supporters rioted, killing a lieutenant. They put his severed head on a pole and carried it around in the streets. In response, the Turkish army called in reinforcements and crushed the uprising, executing Mehmet and the rest of his sleeper cell.

Martin Luther King dismissed those—like the dervish and his disciples—who would fight for a cause with violence as "sleeping through the revolution." He was preoccupied by the question: how to stay awake? Yet sleep itself can be a form of nonviolent resistance, with a revolutionary potential of its own. The Iranian author Kader Abdolah, writing in exile in the Netherlands, begins his novel *My Father's Notebook* with an incantation of the Qur'anic chapter of the Cave. His characters, members of the left-wing opposition to the regime of the shah, Mohammad Reza Pahlavi, and then that of Ayatollah Khomeini, escape from prison and flee into the fictional Saffron Mountain, where they hide in a cave to sleep until Iran is free from tyranny. Their dormancy is a protest, a rejection of everything that has happened in Iran over the course of two repressive governments. "For it is possible to stand up against an unjust system with all of your might, with all of your body, with all of your soul, and yet not stoop to hatred and violence. Something about this approach disarms the opponent. It exposes his moral defenses, weakens his morale, and at the same time, works on his conscience," MLK said. Sleep is just this sort of refusal, contra King: a stance against injustice that is not only nonviolent but as vulnerable, and as noncooperative, as possible. Sleep is an exile found in the dark, an emigration not across borders but time. When governments fail to protect us, the cave steps in.

Fig. 4.2

If the present has become unbearable, the quickest way to get to the future is to sleep. Like a time traveler, but without expensive equipment, the sleeper arrives in the blink of an eye, fresh with memories of the sunken past. In Basra in the late tenth century, a secret society of philosophers who rejected the bloody sectarian conflicts of their age declared themselves the sleepers of the cave. In the aftermath of the murder of the Prophet's family at Karbala in 680, the Ikhwan al-Safa, or Brethren of Purity, imagined—projecting themselves onto the past—that they had chosen to fall asleep and reject as corrupt everything that had subsequently happened in the history of Islam. In their retelling of the sleepers' legend in the *Epistle on Resurrection*, the Brethren took the 309 years revealed by the Qur'an and added forty-five to it, so at the time of its composition their awakening would still lie ahead in the future. They were writing in their sleep.

Sleepers are futurists by nature. Following the publication of *The People of the Cave*, a critic accused Tawfiq al-Hakim of stealing his plot from one of the cult classics of sci-fi. In the weekly paper *Ruz al-Yusuf*, Habib al-Zahlawi published a series of articles claiming that al-Hakim had lifted from the American author Edward Bellamy's 1888 novel *Looking Backward*. A young man falls asleep in Boston in 1887 in his subterranean bedroom, hermetically sealed to shut out the noise of the rapidly industrializing city, rife with poverty and vast inequality. He awakens in the year 2000 into a socialist utopia. The revolution was bloodless: While Julian West slept, the United States abolished capital and private property rights, implemented mandatory labor in service to the nation, and eradicated hunger, laziness, and war. Thousands of readers were convinced. One of the first books in America to sell a million copies, Bellamy's novel persuaded many to become socialists, and some even established utopian communes to bring the book's principles to life. When James B. Weaver ran for president in 1892, the Populist candidate incorporated a number of policies derived from the sleeper story, and attracted a million votes.

Of all the novels, sequels, and satires that the book provoked—one scholar has counted at least sixty-two works indebted to Bellamy published between 1889 and 1900—the best known is H. G. Wells's *When the Sleeper Wakes*. Graham, a desperate insomniac who hasn't slept

for six nights, is on the verge of killing himself
when he finally slips into the sweet, merciful
oblivion. Two hundred and three years later (the
same duration that West slept), Graham awakens
to find that he is the sole owner of a corporation
that, thanks to the logic of compound interest,
has come to own much of the world. While he
dozed, the suffering masses made pilgrimages to
his bedside and prayed that their overlord might
someday be roused to come to their rescue. As
the sleeper peers out over the vastness of future
London, the city he owns, Wells writes, "He
thought of Bellamy, the hero of whose Socialistic
Utopia had so oddly anticipated this actual
experience. But here was no Utopia, no Socialistic
state … the ancient antithesis of luxury, waste and
sensuality on the one hand and abject poverty on
the other, still prevailed."

In the Cairo papers, al-Zahlawi branded
al-Hakim a *mutafalsaf*—an "imitator of
philosophers"—and undertook a point-by-point
comparison of Bellamy's novel and the play. But
he seemed to conclude that the biggest problem
wasn't that al-Hakim had plagiarized, but that he
wasn't plagiarist enough. Al-Zahlawi opined that
the dramatist had let the oxygen of his play go to

waste for failing to use it to promote socialism. Al-Hakim should have used the sleepers to reflect on contemporary social life, the struggle of labor against the exploitation of capital, and the miseries of the *fellahin*, the peasants. "*Looking Backward* is brilliant because it highlights the contrast between two political and social ideas, between socialism and capitalism, through the difference in years," al-Zahlawi wrote, "but what did this author of *The People of the Cave*, may God and Art forgive him, what did he want to show? What was the point of this ruse of three hundred years?" Al-Hakim's play, written at a hopeful moment in Paris in 1928, had appeared in print in 1933 in a morphed world. The Great Depression had plunged Egypt into an economic crisis, tempering the optimism of its Awakening. The new prime minister—a friend of both the Egyptian monarchy and the British—had effectively imposed a dictatorship by suspending the constitution. In such an atmosphere, the dreams of al-Hakim's sleepers seemed empty. Though the playwright was an outspoken critic of the corrupt parliament, the rigged elections, and inert opposition parties, his politics lacked a sense of utopia. That refrain again: *Can't we do better than this?*

In 1958, al-Hakim penned a sci-fi counterpart to *The People of the Cave*. In *Rihlatun ila al-Ghad*, or *Voyage to Tomorrow*, a rocket ship carrying two men—convicts sent as test dummies on an experimental spaceflight—crash-lands on a postapocalyptic planet. When the men miraculously manage to return to Earth, they speculate over how long they have been gone: *a day, part of a day*, they surmise, alluding to the Qur'an. They discover 309 years have passed. The archaic men find themselves in a future in which money no longer exists, everything is always available via machines, and humans no longer need to work. But in such a utopia, life has lost its meaning. The characters speak of how tradition has been sacrificed at the altar of progress, and one of them plots to save humanity from its aimless fate. He ends up silenced in a faraway, prisonlike "City of Quiet" for daring to speak of revolution. (With this play, "the master was permitting himself slightly to nod," one critic wrote.)

Fig. 4.3

In a twelve-minute film made in 2005 in a supermarket in Amsterdam, the Egyptian artist Wael Shawky walks through an endless maze of chilled aisles reciting the *Surat al-Kahf* from memory. Dressed in a blazer and white shirt, he maintains eye contact as he delivers the Qur'anic verses in the relentless monotone of a news report. A digital green news feed races across the bottom of the screen, flashing the English translation of a text incongruous with its surroundings. The Dutch shoppers reflexively filling their baskets barely register the young man's presence. There is no sense as to whether it is day or night in this windowless, fluorescent-lit cavern. The sleepers are time travelers; they are also travelers by air or sea. For Shawky, the story is a parable of immigration, of those who flee their homes to seek better opportunities yet arrive irreparably out of sync on the new shore. He had staged the piece twice before, in supermarkets in Istanbul and Hamburg. The somnolent saints, invoked in the 24–7 labyrinth of potato chips, highlight the strangeness of our dislocated, consumerist age. Should we sleepwalk through it?

"The future is no longer a vague word," al-Hakim decreed in *The Revolt of the Young*, a collection of essays published in 1984, three years before his death. "It is an active moving machine that stands on two feet before us in the image of young people who will live in the year 2000 and beyond." In detailing a slightly vampiric theory of how the young resurrect the past by pumping new blood into it, al-Hakim quoted from the ancient Egyptian *Book of the Dead*. In the text, the god Horus gives new life to the bones of his dead father, Osiris. "Arise, arise, Osiris!" Horus calls, and Osiris shouts, "I am alive!" Al-Hakim, writing in the early years of Hosni Mubarak's thirty-year dictatorship, surmised that Osiris was the homeland Egypt, with its monumental past and its "humiliating present." The playwright, who had always thought of himself as oracular, foresaw that a revolution would be ignited by the young.

In the months following January 4, 2011, the day a twenty-six-year-old street vendor lit himself on fire, an underground art collective calling themselves Ahl al-Kahf—the People of the Cave— took to the streets of Tunis at night. They covered walls and landmarks of the city with collages and stencils: of Mohamed Bouazizi and other martyrs, of Tunisia's ousted president who had fled. Images of army tanks faced off with portraits of Edward Said and Mahmoud Darwish, Qaddafi's head on a rat's body, and aphorisms from Guy Debord. Other symbols were more enigmatic: a man in a gas mask playing an accordion, a procession of nimble black storks. They posted a manifesto on Facebook:

اهل الكهف ليست اشخاص، هي جيل

"al-Kahf" is not an amount of people, it is
a generation

سيخرجون عراة عن التعريف، ابقين عن التوريد

They will emerge multiple, anonymous,
imperceptive and elusive

و سيخرجون من الخراب، و سيخرجون زغاريد

They will emerge from debris, and emerge
as ululations

وسيخرجون زحف شعب طريد

They will emerge, a march of a people
exteriorized

انبياء هامشيون من عصر جديد

marginal prophets from a new era

Fig. 4.4

Every year in July, an unlikely group convenes at a small chapel in Brittany. A mix of Christians and Muslims, they meet to join in prayers at a sixth-century sanctuary devoted to the seven sleepers. In 1954, the year the Algerian War of Independence began, Louis Massignon had the idea for the joint pilgrimage, to deploy syncretism toward peace. He invited a Muslim delegation, largely composed of North Africans in Paris who were confronted daily with racism, to join the age-old crowds of Breton pilgrims at the annual feast in Vieux-Marché. The ritual remains much as it was sixty years ago. On the eve, there is a procession of banners with verses from the Qur'an and images of the Virgin Mary, leading to the *tandad*, the ceremonial bonfire. Mass is said in Arabic, French, and Latin, along with recitations of the *Surat al-Kahf* and a twelfth-century Breton canticle that narrates the tale of the sleepers. Under the shade of chestnut trees, the pilgrims share tea and crepes, milk and dates. A lamb is slaughtered and served with couscous. Near the church, water flows through a granite fountain pierced in seven places. Each year during the war, on the day of the feast, Massignon's friends in Algeria would venture, often at great risk, to pay their respects to the shrine of the sleepers near Sétif, where a stream rushes through a rock in seven channels.

"Let us penetrate into this path that is so wide, in this night that is so dark, into the cave where the Seven Sleepers, who are before God immured in his Holy Will, are cradled in the Dormition of love," Massignon wrote in 1956 to a friend in Cairo. Scholar, soldier, diplomat, mystic, Massignon saw pilgrimage as a political act, able to shift the balance of power through people moving together in space. He was a priest, ordained in the Melkite Church, but Massignon had first experienced transcendence through Islam. He was a prisoner on a ship in Iraq in 1908 when a Stranger had visited him, radiating a phosphorescence like that of a fish. The apparition taught Massignon that history is a chain of witnesses—he believed he was one of them—entering the stage, carrying a truth that is beyond themselves and that runs across the boundaries between religions. Through the Vieux-Marché pilgrimage, Massignon saw a way to create an encounter that would witness the deep bond of this shared story of the sleepers, a link that would make sense only at the End of Days. In the abbey of

Gethsemani in Kentucky, the Trappist monk Thomas Merton fasted in solidarity.

Though states and sects might argue over ownership of the sleepers' cave, for Massignon it was a point within us all. The cave was the center, the *point vierge*: the virgin, innermost cell inside us where we encounter God. It was an idea that the scholar had learned from the ninth-century Sufi martyr al-Hallaj, who described it as a place in our hearts so inaccessible that not even a dream could penetrate it. Taking up the idea from Massignon, Merton called it "the center of our nothingness, where, in apparent despair, one meets God—and is found completely in His mercy." It represents the possibility of escape from oneself by taking refuge within something larger: the point of submission and surrender. It is the site of transformation, of becoming—a dawn state. At the Eranos Conference in August 1939, as Europe hurtled into World War II, C. G. Jung, inspired by the presence of Massignon, composed on the spur of the moment a lecture on the seven sleepers. "The cave is the place of rebirth, that secret cavity in which one is shut up in order to be incubated and renewed," Jung remarked. "Anyone who gets into that cave, that is to say into the cave that everyone has in himself, or into the darkness that lies behind consciousness, will find himself involved in an at first unconscious process of transformation." In the cave, we meet the contents of our unconscious. "This may result in a momentous change of personality in the positive or negative sense," the psychiatrist warned. So, too, on the stage of nations: According to some Islamic schools of oneiromancy, if you dream of seeing Qitmir in a certain country, its ruler or regime will be changed.

July 1962, the month that Algeria gained independence, marked Massignon's last pilgrimage to Vieux-Marché. In a letter dated August 4, he wrote, "For about nine years we have prayed and fasted (eighty-ninth fast last Friday), suffered. *Behold the timid dawn of peace.*" He died a few months later. During this final pilgrimage, Massignon invited the president of the Student Association of Comoros to read the eighteenth sura. "His Arabic psalmody was moving, a cry of resurrection through our seven walled up alive joined with the cry of Magdalene (buried on their threshold) for Lazarus," Massignon recorded. Writes the scholar Anthony O'Mahony, "Resurrection! This was for Massignon the key word." The sleepers, the seven Lazaruses, are among the few to have glimpsed what will happen to us all at the apocalypse. "Their amorous impatience made them appear inordinate, so that they would be witnesses [*of the Resurrection*] for one short moment," Massignon wrote. It is said that their cave is the first place where the trumpet call of Judgment Day will resound. They can't wait.

Fig. 4.5

As for the Hour, there is no doubt concerning it. (18:21)

The earliest record of the word *futurist* is attributed to the Anglican theologian George Stanley Faber, who used it to describe those who believe that the eschatological prophesies of Revelation are still to be fulfilled in the future. When the sleepers awoke in Ephesus, relates Gregory of Tours, they delivered a sermon on the apocalypse to the emperor. "Most august Augustus!" they cried. "In order that you may know that we are all to appear before the judgment seat of Christ according to the words of the Apostle Paul, the Lord God has raised us from the dead and commanded us to make this statement to you. See to it that you are not deceived." Then the witnesses fell back into unconsciousness, to await the Second Coming.

"O, bibliomancer! Know that the People of the Cave have appeared as your augury," reads an inscription in the *Falnama,* a book used to predict the future by sixteenth-century Safavids and Ottomans. One would let the book fall open to a random page, and read the omens conveyed in intricate illustrations and calligraphic forecasts. In the streets of Istanbul or the courts of Isfahan, diviners would help interpret the portents. There were images of the End of Days that did not bode well—hellfire and gigantic scorpions, the scales of Judgment looming over boar-headed traders and men who stole from orphans. But to chance on a picture of the sleepers was felicitous. Qitmir lies coiled at the feet of the saints, who smile, knowingly, in their eternal nap. The augury begins with verses: "I am the dog of the family of Ali, how can I not be safe?" It explains, "The intentions are auspicious; your ascendant appears to be strong; happiness has become your friend." One will accrue wealth and honors (in six days' time), recover lost property, or give birth to a healthy child, the sleepers foretell. In another image, an elusive gray-bearded man with a fiery halo stares into a stream, watching a fish. "Travel is good to the highest degree," it prophesies.

In the eighteenth chapter of the Qur'an, the appearance of the sleepers is followed by an elliptical account of a journey undertaken by Moses, to the place where the two seas meet. Without recognizing it, he and his servant stop at that very place to rest and then continue on. Soon Moses notices that the salted fish they had been carrying for dinner has disappeared. The servant reveals that, at their resting point, he had set the fish down on a rock, but it came back to life, jumped into the sea, and swam away. Moses realizes that they had found the confluence they were seeking. When they return, the fish is gone, but a mysterious Stranger is waiting there.

He is Khidr, the "Green Man," possibly the fish; he is able to appear everywhere and in any guise at any time. He may be a blade of grass, a moth, a flash of phosphorescence. Massignon called him "the director of the Seven Sleepers." He is their watchdog; perhaps he is Qitmir. Moses asks Khidr to teach him the secrets of God's

wisdom, and he reluctantly agrees, taking Moses
on a voyage of initiation. Some say everyone
will encounter Khidr once in their lives: You will
know it if you shake hands with an old, bearded
man missing a bone in his thumb. In Jung's
interpretation, Moses represented the ego while
Khidr was the unconscious self, a figure also
tied to the psychologist's feelings about his father.
In the *Alexander Romance*, Khidr is Alexander
the Great's cook, who drinks the water of life and
attains immortality. Each Friday he prays in
five cities at once. He is on hajj in Mecca but also
in Jerusalem, conversing with the Prophet Elijah.
At the End of Days, he will appear alongside
the Mahdi in battle with the Antichrist, al-Masih
al-Dajjal, to restore justice to the world. Until
then, memorization of the Qur'anic passages
is our amulet: "Whoever learns by heart the first
and last ten verses of *Surat al-Kahf* will become
immune to the evil influence of the Antichrist,"
Muhammad is recorded to have said.

The final episode of the eighteenth relates
how Dhul Qarnayn, "the Two-Horned," identified
with Alexander, travels to the place of the
rising sun. He meets villagers who tell him that
invaders are ravaging the land: Gog and Magog,

peoples from the North. They are the nations
that will rally with Satan, as St. John dreamed in
Revelation, asleep in his Patmos cave. (Gog
is Russia, Reagan said. Gog and Magog are at
work in the Middle East, Bush told Chirac.)
In the Qur'an, Dhul Qarnayn builds a wall of iron
to contain them, a defense that at the eschaton
will be broken, he warns. Since then, it is said
that the wall has been bombarded by shooting
stars thrown by demons and cracked by the
failures of those who sin. Khidr and the apotro-
paic sleepers tirelessly repair it. "The Koran
is pregnant with the future," wrote Norman O.
Brown in 1983.

Think you of the Day when We remove the hills
(18:47)

A stone will loosen. A thorn falls out
of an ear. Heimdallr blows his horn. Mímir's sons
spring up. Mountains will be leveled, leaving
the earth utterly featureless. The dead will float
up from the sea. Each person who has ever lived
will be gathered together; demigods and mythic
creatures herded into a separate pen. The books
that leave out nothing will be opened. Jerusalem
will come down from heaven styled like a bride.
The sleepers are amorously impatient.

5. Resurrection

*Can you imagine what it's like for a man to be
resurrected from the sleep of death after years
and generations have passed, during which all the
reasons for living, for hope, have changed? How do
you think you would handle the situation?*
　　　　　　　　—Al-Ahram review of *The People
　　　　　　　　　　of the Cave*, December 18, 1935

*lights have entered
us it is a music more powerful
than music
till other voices wake
us or we drown*
　　　　　　　　— George Oppen's transformation
　　　　　　　　　　of a line from T. S. Eliot

In the final scene of Tawfiq al-Hakim's *The People
of the Cave,* the princess Priska realizes that she
is in love with Mishlinya, that mariner wrecked
on the shores of time, the man who loved her
ancestor. Mishlinya had finally come to his senses,
after a heated argument with the princess, and
realized that three centuries had passed, and that

she was a different Priska. In despair, he fled the palace, to join the other sleepers back in the cave. As if moving by the propulsion of some prophecy, the princess waits for a month to pass and then goes to visit the cave, assuming that by now he must be dead. She becomes hysterical when she finds Mishlinya alive—he was waiting for her—yet on the verge of slipping away. She commands the tutor Gallias to bring milk in haste to resuscitate him, but it is too late. "You resurrected for me, and I was resurrected for you," she tells Mishlinya. "Till we meet again," the sleeper says. Unaware that his daughter is within, the king orders the cave to be ceremoniously sealed, to protect the bodies. In a dramatic ending, Priska chooses to remain in the sepulcher, and join Mishlinya in the long, sweet annihilation.

Perhaps her decision isn't so mad. What do we know of death? Perhaps there persists some remnant of heat and life, some trace of one's original form. A spark—or is it a dream?—still smolders between them. Perhaps love is a law of affinity between molecules, atoms that recombine with each other over the centuries in whatever way they can. The moldering lovers await the next resurrection. Pickaxes are left on the inside of the cave, just in case, at some point in the deep future, the sleepers need to break through to the light.

Fig. 5.1

A thirty-two-year-old man was escorted by the police to the emergency room of the Bakırköy Psychiatric Hospital in Istanbul, records a case study from 2011 by a team of four Turkish psychologists. He had been found with his three young children, locked inside a room with his pregnant wife's decaying corpse. She was not dead, he stated in an interrogation. She was sleeping. She would soon resurrect.

The man had worked as a teacher, his wife as an architect. After they married, they quit their jobs and cut all social ties, choosing to spend their days reading the Qur'an. The wife gave birth to two children. The couple began to share delusions that they were being persecuted for their faith. Fearing that they would become contaminated by contact with infidels, they moved from Istanbul to another province. They had another child. Financial difficulties forced them to move in with the husband's family. Soon after they arrived, they began acting strangely. They shut themselves and the children into a room, and refused to speak to the rest of the household. They had their meals delivered to their door. When the husband's parents confronted them, the couple grew defensive, claimed they were being hounded for their faith, and fled.

The couple moved in with the wife's parents, and again locked themselves and their children in a room. They would read the Qur'an by letting the pages fall open to random verses. Often, the book chose to open to the *Surat al-Kahf*, and they would dwell on the line, *They sheltered in a cave.* During the night, they would retrieve the meals that were left outside the door only if they landed on the verse, *They sent one of them out to bring food.* If not, they didn't eat. One day the wife became contorted by pain and began to cry out, and then her body went cold. The man interpreted it as a line from the Sura of Sad: *We questioned Solomon and left him on the ground as a corpse.* In the chapter, King Solomon is reduced to a "skeleton on a throne" by God as a test of his devotion, and then resurrected. The husband left his wife's body to be, on the assumption that she would soon wake.

After ten days without communication from the couple, the wife's family, hearing the sounds of the children weeping, broke down the door. The room was covered in blood and shit, the wife was dead, and the children were on the verge of starvation. An autopsy determined that she had been four months pregnant, miscarried, and died from loss of blood. Her husband said: "She fell asleep for a period like the People of the Cave. She was going to wake up and deliver the fourth baby followed by three others—the seven sleepers." She must not be buried, he protested. The husband was hospitalized, given clozapine, and released from custody.

Two years later, the man remarried, and his children, who had been under the care of relatives, moved back in with him. He stopped taking the clozapine. He began to relocate from place to place with his family, believing that they were being persecuted for their faith. He began sending apocalyptic messages from his phone. He locked his new wife and the children into a room. She escaped through the window.

Fig. 5.2

In 1971, Tawfiq al-Hakim, "an Egyptian more than
five thousand years old," as he called himself,
returned to Paris, the site of his education in the
theater. With his trademark beret and walking
stick, al-Hakim went to visit the neighborhood
where he had once lived, forty-five years earlier.
He couldn't find the restaurant where he used
to eat lunch. He asked a policeman to direct him
to Rue Pelleport, the quiet street where he had
once resided. But even the street now went in a
different direction. It had been transformed into a
wide, bustling commercial avenue, traversing a
new diagonal of the city, and had its own metro.
The former Rue Pelleport had been renamed. His
old house was gone. Baffled, al-Hakim stopped
passersby in the street to ask where to find the
landmarks he remembered, but he received
nothing but confusion in response. "It was as
though I had turned into a character from *The
People of the Cave*," he said, in an interview in
Al-Ahram. "How can the playwright become a

character in his own play? … Writers are used to living life first and then writing it. But in many instances, I write life and then I live it afterward. And *now I fear what I write*, scared that I am writing my fate with my own hands."

"Arise, arise!" al-Hakim once wrote, channeling the bird-god Horus. The playwright told of awakenings. Now no one sleeps anymore. The nightly sleeper, before the onset of industrialization, dozed ten hours an evening on average. Now we cultivate insomnia, a kind of vigilance against the violence of the world that is always on digital display. Time moves at the speed of the information we scroll through in the night. We live in 24–7 time, a cosmos where the distinction between night and day shrinks, where age-old circadian rhythms have given way to a block of undifferentiated moments, lit by the glow of energy-saving bulbs and the ever-open signs of e-commerce. As the theorist Jonathan Crary writes, this world created by capitalism is "a world with the shallowest of pasts, and thus in principle without specters. But the homogeneity of the present is an effect of the fraudulent brightness that presumes to extend everywhere and to preempt any mystery or unknowability." Sleep remains a lone site of resistance, the last mystery that defies exposure. In recent years, the US Department of Defense has directed considerable resources into studying the brain of the white-crowned sparrow. On its yearly migration it is able to fly for seven days without sleeping, without suffering any loss in cognitive function. If its secret is unlocked, the hope is that soldiers, and someday civilians, could be trained to imitate the wakeful bird.

"There exists only the instant," Massignon remarked in a lecture he gave at the Eranos Conference in 1951. "For the Muslim theologian time is not a continuous 'duration,' but a con-stellation, a 'galaxy' of instants," he argued, citing scholars such as the eleventh-century Sufi mystic al-Qushayri. It is a physics not unlike that of 24–7 time, with its instant gratifications documented and shared instantaneously. In such a cosmos, Massignon explained, only the moment exists, for every atom is created anew at every second. There is no necessary connection between cause and effect—between them lies only the inscrutable will of God. The most profound instant in the Islamic calendar occurs at twilight, with the appearance of the new moon. "It is not permissible to foresee the new moon by means of theoretical tables," Massignon related. "It must be watched for and established by two 'witnesses of the instant.'" The tenth-century jurist ibn al-Qass argued that the sun's movement is discontinuous: Each night it retreats to a resting place, which it will leave only at God's command. There is no certainty that the future will resemble the past. This is good news, or terrifying.

The supremacy of the instant is visible in the form of the Qur'an itself, the book that descended to earth in what is known as the Night of Power. Nonlinear, seemingly out of joint, it has the texture of interruption. *To God belong the secrets of the heavens and the earth, and the matter of the Hour is as the twinkling of an eye, or it is nearer still*, it reveals (16:77). The twinkling or the blink of an eye, *lamh al-basar*, is the instant. "The heresiographers condemn as materialists the 'Dahriyun,' the philosophers who divinize Duration (*dahr*)," wrote Massignon. At best, duration is the silent interval between two instants, what elapses between lightning and thunder. One must not worship it. At the Hour, the galaxy of moments will be gathered together. "The instant is a pearl-bearing shell, sealed at the bottom of the ocean of a human heart," said the martyr al-Hallaj, as recorded by Attar. "Tomorrow, at the rising tide of Judgment, all the shells will be cast on the beach; and we shall see if any pearl emerges from them." The apocalypse will be an indescribably large collection of seashells.

Perhaps in the end there is no story of the seven sleepers, because duration means nothing. What is 187 years; what is 309? Time exists only in the instant. Continuity between one point and the next is upheld by God, or by a force even more unfathomable. "History becomes a night, or seven nights," wrote Norman O. Brown. That the world is made anew every moment is the logic of 24–7 capitalism and Sufi metaphysics, but it is also the logic of the dream, in which a century can pass in the instant between flipping from one's right side to one's left. If the story fails, make it new. Revolution begins with reverie. Mundane sleep is the nightly rehearsal, as Crary writes, "of what more consequential renewals and beginnings might be." The *Surat al-Kahf* concludes with the penultimate verse, *Say: Though the sea became ink for the Words of my Lord, verily the sea would be used up before the Words of my Lord were exhausted.* (18:109) Sleep is a surface like the sea, an ink to draft what is to come. We write life, and we live it afterward.

Fig. 5.3

They sleep in al-Qarafa. They sleep in the cemetery at Pordic. They sleep in Zincirlikuyu, under a shopping mall. They are on their way to the future. The sleeper reaches out a decomposing finger and beckons, *Join us.*

Sources
(In the order in which they appear)

1

Roger Allen, *A Period of Time: A Study of Muhammad Al-Muwaylihi's "Hadith 'Isa ibn Hisham"* (Middle East Centre, St. Antony's College Oxford, Reading, UK: Ithaca Press, 1992).

Tawfiq al-Hakim, *The People of the Cave* (Ahl al-Kahf), trans. Mahmoud El Lozy (Cairo: Elias Modern Publishing House, 1989). I have made some small edits to the translation throughout.

Ramsis Awad, ed., *Madha qallu 'an Ahl al-Kahf* (Cairo: Al-Hay'a al-'Amma al-Misriyya li al-Kitab, 1986). I am indebted to Raphael Cormack for discovering this book in a library in Khartoum and photocopying it for me. Many thanks to Hussein Omar for his translation of this and other Arabic sources throughout the piece.

Muhammad Mustafa Badawi, ed., *The Cambridge History of Modern Arabic Literature* (Cambridge, UK: Cambridge University Press, 1992), chapters 9 and 10.

Tawfiq al-Hakim, *The Prison of Life*, trans. Pierre Cachia (Cairo: American University in Cairo Press, 1992).

Dina Amin, "Tawfiq al-Hakim," in *Essays in Arabic Literary Biography: 1850–1950*, ed. Roger M. A. Allen, Joseph Edmund Lowry, and Devin J. Stewart (Wiesbaden: Harrassowitz, 2010), 98–112.

Richard Long, *Tawfiq al-Hakim, Playwright of Egypt* (London: Ithaca Press, 1979).

Pierre Cachia, "Idealism and Ideology: The Case of Tawfiq al-Hakim," *Journal of the American Oriental Society* 100, no. 3 (July–October 1980), 225–35.

William M. Hutchins, *Tawfiq Al-Hakim: A Reader's Guide* (Boulder, CO: L. Rienner, 2003).

Tawfiq al-Hakim, *The Return of the Spirit*, trans. William M. Hutchins (Washington, DC: Three Continents Press, 1990).

Paul Starkey, "Philosophical Themes in Tawfiq al-Hakim's Drama," *Journal of Arabic Literature* 8 (1977), 136–52.

William M. Hutchins, "The Theology of Tawfiq al-Hakim: An Exposition with Examples," *The Muslim World* 78, nos. 3–4 (1988), 243–79.

Bruce Fudge, "The Men of the Cave: Tafsir, Tragedy and Tawfiq al-Hakim," *Arabica* 54, no. 1 (January 2007), 67–93.

Paul Starkey, *From the Ivory Tower: A Critical Study of Tawfiq al-Hakim* (London: Ithaca Press, 1987).

Richard Long, "Tawfiq al-Hakim and the Arabic Theatre," *Middle Eastern Studies* 5, no. 1 (January 1969), 69–74.

Gilbert Victor Tutungi, "Tawfiq al-Hakim and the West" (PhD diss., Indiana University, 1966).

Al-Ahram newspaper, articles from December 18, 1935; November 29, 1968; August 6, 1971; and August 13, 1971.

2

Muhammad Marmaduke Pickthall, *The Meaning of the Glorious Qur'an* (Hyderabad, India: Government Central Press, 1938).

A. J. Arberry, *The Qur'an Interpreted* (London: George Allen & Unwin, 1955).

Tarif Khalidi, trans., *The Qur'an* (London: Penguin Books: 2008).

Sayyid Qutb, *In the Shade of the Qur'an* (Fi Zilal al-Qur'an), vol. 11, trans. Adil Salahi (Leicestershire, UK; Islamic Foundation, 2003), 182–203.

Maulana Abul Kalam Azad, *The Tarjuman al-Quran*, vol. 3, trans. Syed Abdul Latif (Hyderabad, India: Trust for Qur'anic Cultural Research, Da'iratu'l Ma'arif Press, 1978).

S. A. Kamali, "Abul Kalam Azad's Commentary on the Qur'an," *The Muslim World* 49, no. 1 (1959), 518.

Sebastian Brock, "Jacob of Serugh's Poem on the Sleepers of Ephesus," in *"I Sowed Fruits into Hearts" (Odes Sol. 17:13): Festschrift for Professor Michael Lattke*, ed. P. Allen, M. Franzmann, and R. Strelan (Early Christian Studies 12; Strathfield, Australia: St. Pauls Publications, 2007), 13–30.

Pieter W. Van der Horst, "Pious Long-Sleepers in Pagan, Jewish, and Christian Antiquity," in *Studies in Ancient Judaism and Early Christianity* (Leiden, Netherlands: Brill, 2014), 248–66.

Richard F. Burton, *The Book of the Thousand Nights and a Night*, vol. 3 (New York: Heritage Press, 1934).

Edward Gibbon, *The History of the Decline and Fall of the Roman Empire,* vol. 3, ed. J. B. Bury (London: Methuen, 1909), III: 436–39.

Sidney Griffith, "Christian Lore and the Arabic Qur'an: The 'Companions of the Cave' in *Surat al-Kahf* and in Syriac Christian Tradition," in *The Qur'an in Its Historical Context*, ed. Gabriel Said Reynolds (Oxford, UK: Routledge, 2008), 109–38.

Norman Oliver Brown, *Apocalypse and/or Metamorphosis* (Berkeley: University of California Press, 1991).

Ernest Honigmann, "Stephen of Ephesus (April 15, 448–Oct. 29, 451) and the Legend of the Seven Sleepers," in *Patristic Studies*, vol. 173, Studi e Testi (Città del Vaticano: Biblioteca Apostolica Vaticana, 1953), 125–68.

Antigone Samellas, *Death in the Eastern Mediterranean (50–600 AD): The Christianization of the East* (Tübingen, Germany: Mohr Siebeck, 2002).

3.

Clive Foss, *Ephesus After Antiquity: A Late Antique, Byzantine, and Turkish City* (Cambridge, UK: Cambridge University Press, 1979).

Mark Twain, "The Legend of the Seven Sleepers," in *Innocents Abroad* (Hartford, CT: American Publishing Co., 1869).

Louis Massignon, "Les Sept Dormants, Apocalypse de l'Islam" and "Le culte liturgique et populaire des VII Dormants martyrs d'Ephèse (Ahl al-kahf): Trait d'union orient-occident entre l'Islam et la Chrétienté," in *Opera Minora,* vol. 3 (Paris: Presses Universitaires de France, 1969), 104–80.

Dorothy C. Buck, "A Shared Muslim-Christian Pilgrimage," *Sufi: A Journal of Sufism*, no. 65 (Spring 2005), 20–23.

Michael Huber, *Die Wanderlegende von den Siebenschläfern* (Leipzig, Germany: O. Harrassowitz, 1910).

Louis Dupree, "Functions of Folklore in Afghan Society," *Asian Affairs* 10, no. 1 (1979), 51–61.

Guy Le Strange, *Palestine Under the Moslems: A Description of Syria and the Holy Land from AD 650 to 1500* (London: Alexander P. Watt, 1890).

Oya Pancaroglu, "Caves, Borderlands and Configurations of Sacred Topography in Medieval Anatolia," *Mésogeios* 25–26 (2005), 249–81.

Viktor Rydberg, *Teutonic Mythology: Gods and Goddesses of the Northland*, vol. 3, trans. Rasmus B. Anderson (London: Norroena Society, 1906).

Frank Barlow, ed. and trans., *The Life of King Edward Who Rests at Westminster, Attributed to a Monk of St. Bertin* (London: Thomas Nelson and Sons, 1962).

Tewfik Canaan, "The Decipherment of Arabic Talismans," in *Magic and Divination in Early Islam*, ed. Emilie Savage-Smith (Aldershot: Ashgate, 2004), 125–77.

Venetia Porter, "Amulets Inscribed with the Names of the 'Seven Sleepers' of Ephesus in the British Museum," in *Word of God, Art of Man: The Qur'an and Its Creative Expressions*, ed. Fahmida Suleman (Oxford, UK: Oxford University Press, 2007), 123–34.

Sabine Baring-Gould, *Curious Myths of the Middle Ages* (Boston: Little Brown, 1904).

Jaf'ar Sharif, *Qanoon-e-Islam, or the Customs of the Moosulmans of India; comprising a Full and Exact Account of Their Various Rites and Ceremonies, from the Moment of Birth till the Hour of Death*, trans. G. A. Herklots (London: Parbury, Allen, and Co., 1832).

Craig Crossen and Stephan Prochazka, "The Seven Sleepers and Ancient Constellation Traditions—a Crossover of Arabic Dialectology with the History of Astronomy," *Wiener Zeitschrift für die Kunde des Morgenlandes* 97 (2007), 79–105.

Danilo Kiš, *The Encyclopedia of the Dead*, trans. Michael Henry Heim (New York: Farrar, Straus and Giroux, 1989).

Emine Gürsoy-Naskali, *Ashabu 'l-Kahf: A Treatise in Eastern Turki* (Helsinki: Suomalais-Ugrilainen Seura, 1985).

4.

Rev. Dr. Martin Luther King Jr., "Remaining Awake Through a Great Revolution" (commencement address for Oberlin College, Oberlin, Ohio, June 14, 1965).

Washington Irving, *The Legend of Sleepy Hollow and Other Stories* (New York: Penguin Classics, 2014).

Christine Philliou, "When the Clock Strikes Twelve: The Inception of an Ottoman Past in Early Republican Turkey," *Comparative Studies of South Asia, Africa, and the Middle East* 31, no. 1 (2011), 172–82.

Umut Azak, "A Reaction to Authoritarian Modernization in Turkey: The Menemen Incident and the Creation and Contestation of a Myth, 1930–1931," in *The State and the Subaltern: Modernization, Society and the State in Turkey and Iran*, ed. Touraj Atabaki (London: I. B. Tauris, 2007), 143–58.

Kader Abdolah, *My Father's Notebook*, trans. Susan Massotty (New York: Harper Perennial, 2006).

Godefroid de Callataÿ, "Astrology and Prophecy: The Ikhwan al-Safa and the Legend of the Seven Sleepers," in Charles Burnett et al., *Studies in the History of the Exact*

Sciences in Honour of David Pingree (Boston: Brill, 2004), 758–85.

Edward Bellamy, *Looking Backward: 2000–1887*, ed. Matthew Beaumont (Oxford, UK: Oxford University Press, 2009).

H. G. Wells, *When the Sleeper Wakes* (New York: Harper & Bros., 1899).

Tawfiq al-Hakim, "Voyage to Tomorrow," in *Plays, Prefaces & Postscripts of Tawfiq al-Hakim*, vol. 2, trans. William M. Hutchins (Washington, DC: Three Continents Press, 1984).

———, *The Revolt of the Young: Essays by Tawfiq al-Hakim*, trans. Mona Radwan (Syracuse, NY: Syracuse University Press, 2014).

Anthony O'Mahony, "Louis Massignon, the Seven Sleepers of Ephesus and the Christian-Muslim pilgrimage at Vieux-Marché, Brittany," in *Explorations in a Christian Theology of Pilgrimage*, ed. Craig Bartholomew and Fred Hughes (Aldershot, UK: Ashgate, 2004), 126–48.

Louis Massignon, "Visitation of the Stranger: Response to an Inquiry about God" (1955), in *Testimonies and Reflections: Essays of Louis Massignon*, ed. Herbert Mason (South Bend, IN: University of Notre Dame Press, 1989).

Patrick Laude and Edin Q. Lohja, *Louis Massignon: The Vow and the Oath* (London: Matheson Trust, 2011).

Sidney H. Griffith, "Thomas Merton, Louis Massignon, and the Challenge of Islam," *The Merton Annual* 3 (1990), 151–74.

Carl Gustav Jung, "A Typical Set of Symbols Illustrating the Process of Transformation," in *The Archetypes and the Collective Unconscious*, trans. R. F. C. Hull (Princeton, NJ: Bollingen Series, Princeton University Press, 1990), 135–50.

Farhad Massumeh, ed., *Falnama: The Book of Omens* (London: Thames & Hudson, 2009).

Nicholas Battye, "Khidr in the Opus of Jung: The Teaching of Surrender," in *Jung and the Monotheisms: Judaism, Christianity, and Islam*, ed. Joel Ryce-Menuhin (London: Routledge, 1994).

5.

George Oppen, "Till Other Voices Wake Us," in *New Collected Poems,* ed. Michael Davidson (New York: New Directions, 2002), 286.

Menekse Sila Yazar, Evrim Erbek, Nezih Eradamlar and Latif Alpkan, "The Seven Sleepers: A folie à deux case originating from a religious-cultural belief," *Transcultural Psychiatry* 48 (2011), 684–92.

Jonathan Crary, *24/7: Late Capitalism and the Ends of Sleep* (New York: Verso, 2013).

Louis Massignon, "Time in Islamic Thought" (1955), trans. Ralph Manheim, in *Man and Time: Papers from the Eranos Yearbooks*, ed. Joseph Campbell (New York: Princeton University Press, 1983).

Figures

Fig. 1.1
A man rises from his grave in the Egyptian satirical newspaper *Abou Naddara*, published by James Sanua in Paris in 1878. Courtesy of Heidelberg University.

Fig. 1.2
The Khedivial Opera House in the year it first opened in Cairo, 1869.
Photographer unknown. Courtesy of the Bibliotheca Alexandrina.

Fig. 1.3
Mahmoud Mukhtar's statue of the Nahdat Misr, or "The Awakening
of Egypt," in Cairo. Photograph by Lesley Lababidi. Courtesy of the
photographer.

Fig. 1.4
Shadows in a cave. Photographer unknown.

Fig. 2.1
A sixteenth-century Persian manuscript illustration of the Seven Sleepers
and their dog, from Ishaq ibn Ibrahim al-Nishapuri's *Qisas al-Anbiya'*, or
"Legends of the Prophets." Courtesy of the Spencer Collection at the New
York Public Library.

Fig. 2.2
A Russian icon of the Seven Sleepers of Ephesus, ca. 1800. Courtesy of the
Mark Gallery, London.

Fig. 2.3
A manuscript illustration of the Seven Sleepers from the Persian historian Rashid al-Din's monumental *Jami' al-Tawarikh*, or "Compendium of Chronicles," early fourteenth century. Courtesy of the University of Edinburgh.

Fig. 4.1
An aerial view of the outskirts of the cave and mosque of the Seven
Sleepers in Amman, Jordan. Courtesy of the Aerial Photographic Archive
for Archaeology in the Middle East.

Fig. 4.2
Henri Lanos, "Graham awakens unexpectedly," 1899. Illustration of a scene from H. G. Wells's *When the Sleeper Wakes* (1899). Courtesy of Leo Boudreau.

Fig. 4.3
Alaa Awad and Ammar Abu-Bakr, mural on Muhammad Mahmoud Street,
Cairo, September 2012. Photograph by Nancy Demerdash.

Fig. 4.4
Louis Massignon and the leader of the Comoros Student Association
read the Qur'an at the pilgrimage to the Seven Sleepers in Vieux-Marché,
Brittany, 1962. Photograph by Louis-Claude Duchesne.

Fig. 4.5
Inside the cave of the Seven Sleepers in Amman, a scene from the "Voices of Religious Tolerance" conference, cohosted by the US Marine Corps and the government of Afghanistan in April 2011. Photograph by Lance Corporal Richard Sanglap-Heram.

Fig. 5.1
The Seven Sleepers in an illumination from the German manuscript *The Passionary of Weissenau*, late twelfth century. Courtesy of Fondation Martin Bodmer.

Fig. 5.2
King Edward receives a vision of seven men asleep in a cave in Ephesus.
Anglo-Norman manuscript illustration from *The Life of St. Edward
the Confessor*, written in England ca. 1250. Courtesy of the University
of Cambridge.

Fig. 5.3
Two deer and a fox visit the Seven Sleepers in an Alsatian manuscript
illustration, ca. 1418. Courtesy of the University of Heidelberg.

The Long Tomorrow

Not Dead But Sleeping is part of The Long Tomorrow; an issue that asks: Who bears the responsibility, and who possesses the imaginative capacity, to conceive of an ideal world? Though utopians, futurists, and visionaries have never been united under one standard, radicals and progressives used to be uniquely equipped and motivated to do this work, and today mostly defend the scraps of bygone idealism and attend to the detritus of twentieth-century achievements. But constructing an image of an alternative world, another way of living, has an essential social function, and reflects—or even determines—the agency of the constructors. This task, like forming an image of the past, is never neutral or impartial. And now those who make investments in the future—and whose investments pay off—tend to be libertarian technologists, financial engineers, and affiliates of plutocrat-funded think tanks. This issue is an exhortation to bet on the future again—to formulate propositions, predictions, and projections that make demands on the present.

Read more, including a table of contents, here: canopycanopycanopy.com/issues/21

Triple Canopy is a magazine based in New York. Since 2007, Triple Canopy has advanced a model for publication that encompasses digital works of art and literature, public conversations, exhibitions, and books. This model hinges on the development of publishing systems that incorporate networked forms of production and circulation. Working closely with artists, writers, technologists, and designers, Triple Canopy produces projects that demand considered reading and viewing. Triple Canopy resists the atomization of culture and, through sustained inquiry and creative research, strives to enrich the public sphere. Triple Canopy is a nonprofit 501(c)(3) organization and a member of Common Practice New York.

Not Dead But Sleeping was published as part of Triple Canopy's Research Work project area, which receives support from the Andy Warhol Foundation for the Visual Arts, the Brown Foundation, Inc., of Houston, the Lambent Foundation Fund of Tides Foundation, and the New York City Department of Cultural Affairs in partnership with the City Council.

The author also received support from the Tamaas Foundation and Dar al-Ma'mûn in Marrakech. She would like to thank Sarah Riggs, Omar Berrada, Juan Asís Palao Gómez, all the staff at DAM, Khalil Nemmaoui, and Nathaniel Tarn.